BE YOU

A JOURNEY TO SELF TRANSFORMATION

KULSOOM KAZIM

Published by Iron Heart Publishing House.

www.ironheartpublishing.com

I dedicate this book to my Lord, the One who created me and has showered His infinite blessing upon me, my mom who has been the model of a strong woman for me, and my husband without whom this could not have been possible.

I also dedicate this book to all the individuals who are ever struggling through those simple things in life. To everyone who has had or is having a bad day. I dedicate these words to those who have lost hope, and I promise to try, in my full capacity, to lift you back up.

Contents

INTRODUCTION

In the name of Allah, the Most Gracious,
the Most Merciful

I wrote this book with you in my thoughts.
Yes, you.

I believe that we all sail the same boat. We
bear the same struggles, the same pain, and
same confusions...just different flavors.

In my own journey as a woman, a life coach,
and an influencer, I have reflected on my
own trials. I have watched my life unfold in
a manner which has, at times, left me in awe,
tears, silence, and an opportunity for me to

learn and grow. Throughout my life, I have felt sorrow and ache for the pain that people feel. I have longed to help people reach their full potential because the smiles on their faces are precious. It is for this reason that I became a life coach and an influencer, so that I may work closely with women all around the world and continue to inspire them.

I also have a deep passion for Islam, hence my endless pursuit of attaining knowledge continues. I believe nothing is possible without carrying Islamic values and thus I find it crucial to instill those same morals and values in the work I do and the people I meet. As a life coach, I have come across many women who have experienced heart-breaking trials-from serenity to abuse and suicidal thoughts, from marriage to divorce, from financial independence to instability.

Even in the midst of all these trials, I have found these women to have extraordinary goals and exceptional visions. I therefore find it my duty and moral obligation to work with them and help them, so that they may achieve their goals and in turn give back to the *Ummah*.

We ought to live a manner which enables us to be in service to others, but one cannot be successful in such endeavors when they haven't worked on themselves at the basic levels. As such, my aim in this book is to help you work on yourself using methods which I have tried and consciously worked on, and continue to pursue every day.

On this journey of life, of you being 'you', you may be befuddled about your vision. You may be concerned about your decisions, your goals, and ambitions. You may be rekindling your relationship with your loved ones. Your friends and family. Your Creator, Allah the Exalted- He who has breathed life in every one of us. The One who created us all. It could be that you want to relive the happiness in your relationships with others. Perhaps you are stranded in the efforts of taking care of others, and so you lose yourself in their endeavors, or your confidence sinks to such depths, that it seems 'you' may never be found. I understand this and therefore, I believe it is of utmost importance to align yourself with Allah, your vision, relationships, self-care, and confidence, to become the best you that this world has ever seen. I find that these five aspects are very important aspects in terms of the foundations we ought to build and actively work on.

I have broken down each aspect into a unique chapter for you to understand and ponder on. I have incorporated stories from my own life and from those unique individuals I have met along the way. There are exercises to help you take actionable steps and reflective questions for those days you want to sit and contemplate in silence.

I firmly believe that working on these aspects will help you in your true purpose in this world – serving Islam and being a true leader. I am aware that there are many more things one may work on, however, from my experience I find that these five are the most common themes that always come up in life.

Whatever ordeal you are facing, I can assure you, you do not sail alone.

We share the same boat. I too have faced my share of burdens and struggles, hardships sent my way by the very essences of life, and I am prepared to share these struggles with you.

I hope to relate some exhilarating aspects of my life and the lives of some of the most inspirational folks I have met along the way.

Most importantly, I want to challenge and provoke you through my words, with the hopes of helping you find those life-changing solutions you have sought for so long.

If anything I have said has hit home, touched your heart, and triggered an inner sense of intuition, then keep reading. I want to teach you to be the best 'you' that you can be, and prepare you to conquer all that you hope to conquer in life.

I will walk every mile with you. I will sail to the furthest seas with you. I will never abandon you. I will listen. I will empathize, and you can always reach out to me for a helping hand.

This, I promise.

Humbly and Sincerely,
Kulsoom Kazim

ALLAH

Ponder upon the reality that Allah is all that you really have.

MY ONE CHOICE

We are bound by the choices we make. Sometimes they are good and sometimes they are bad, but in all walks of life, they test us.

I often ask myself, "What are those fleeting thoughts clouding our minds before we make those critical decisions in life? What drives our choices?"

As we make certain choices, we face the consequences of those choices. The consequences of pain and regret, pleasure and happiness. Those choices then remain in our storybook forever. They shape us. They define us. Those who are wise will seek to make beneficial choices, while those who fail to acquire this wisdom will face the negative consequences.

I want to share two very special moments with you, when I found myself at crossroads with important decisions to make. The two moments which changed my life, and I can happily say they were wise choices. It is these moments that have brought me closer to Allah (*Subhanahu-Wa-Ta'ala*) forever. They have helped me be in harmony with myself, the world and my Creator.

If you look at me, you may think that I obeyed Allah's commands all my life, but I assure you that is not the case. I struggled, like many, to fulfill my obligations. I did not tolerate anyone dictating my life because I believed we live in a world which encourages freedom of choice and liberation.

This is a widely misunderstood concept, because while we have the freedom to say and do as we please, we are still humans who are limited in our thought and ability, and hence we are prone to making mistakes. Our liberation then comes from the One who is perfect – Allah (*Subhanahu-Wa-Ta'ala*). We live in a world where doing bad is easier than doing good. A world where being religious doesn't meet the status quo.

I once fell into that trap. I made my own choices and made mistakes. I disobeyed Allah's simple command to pray. How I could have been so ungrateful, I still don't know, but I do know that now, with every force in my body, I will do everything I can to worship my Lord. Because I owe utmost gratitude to Him for sending me to this world, choosing me to do good and showing me mercy even when I wouldn't have mercy on myself. It is not about being individualistic, but rather realizing that we are slaves to Allah, and being at peace and alignment with this is where our success lies. Realizing that we are imperfect, and He is not, will save us from arrogance. Realizing that He is Wise, while we have fault, will allow us to fully understand His majestic nature.

Allah (Subhanahu-Wa-Ta'ala) says in Soorah Luqman, Ayah 12 of the Qur'an: "Anyone who is grateful, does so to the profit of his own soul".

The sooner we realize this, the sooner we can live a life with true purpose, hence pleasing Allah. Living in gratitude is indeed an excellent way to live. It humbles us and liberates us. It leaves us at the doorstep of the Most Merciful Lord who will never let us down.

We all have pivotal moments in our life when we make a choice which remains with us forever. For me, it was the *Hijab*. I actively began praying and wearing proper *Hijab* as I crossed over my teenage years into adulthood. I have never since gone back, and now I understand the importance of obeying Allah's every command. I understand what commitment means. I understand that freedom of choice doesn't come from me, because as a human I am imperfect. I understand what it means to love someone more than yourself, and I am able to make sense of the fact that my *Hijab* is, in fact, my liberation, not a nuisance which I indifferently accepted before.

"You always talk about religion, so why don't you just wear the *Hijab*?" she asked.

She was a friend, very honest and straightforward. Her question, at the time, irritated me because I simply did not know the answer. Have you ever felt this unease, when you are doing something wrong and you know in your heart that it is wrong, yet you justify it in every humane way possible?

Her question made me uneasy about the fact that I wasn't adorning the *Hijab* as I should have. The fact that I was disobedient to Allah, and were I to have died that day, or even today, there would be no redemption for me. The discomfort I found in her questions heightened my frustrations. I had that desire, yet the rebel in me was also quite strong. How could I force myself to do what I want? I envied the girls who wore *Hijab*, because deep down, I knew they were doing something right. I was living a life of denial because I knew I ought to be doing something and yet I was making every excuse not to.

All through high school, I, like many teenagers, yearned to fit into society. I prayed on *Eid* and random days. I knew the bare minimum about what was required of me. But one thing was for sure, I always knew I was doing something wrong. I longed for more. It was as if there was a void in my heart. The *Hijab* always attracted me. I loved fasting. I would secretly make *Dua* to Allah, asking Him to bring me closer to Him, and I wasn't exactly sure why I even wanted that. I always felt unease when I committed sin, and now, years later, as I reflect on my condition, I recall the words of our beloved Prophet (peace be upon him).

"On the authority of Wabisah bin Ma'bad (may Allah be pleased with him) who said: 'I came to the Messenger of Allah and he said "You have come to ask about righteousness." I said, "Yes." He said, "Consult your heart. Righteousness is that about which the soul feels at ease and the

heart feels tranquil. And wrongdoing is that which wavers in the soul and causes uneasiness in the breast, even though people have repeatedly given their legal opinion."

[40 Hadith Nawawi: #27. A good hadeeth transmitted from the Musnads of the two imams, Ahmed bin Hanbal and Al-Darimi with a good chain of authorities]

Pondering on this hadith I realized the beauty of our hearts. We feel it in our hearts and core when we do something wrong so how could I have been at ease all those years knowing that I was disobeying Allah (*Subhanahu-Wa-Ta'ala*)?

I always told myself that I wanted to fix my inner self, my inner *Hijab*, before adopting the outer *Hijab*, which I realize now, was a limitation in my thinking. Working on our inner-selves is extremely important, however, we must not forget that the external is also an obligation upon us. How will we answer to Allah (*Subhanahu-Wa-Ta'ala*) knowing that we are not fulfilling one of His commands? It may be challenging and anxiety-reckoning at times. This we cannot deny.

The struggle is real. I have seen it in the

eyes of many women. They have cried tears of pain and hurt, unable to face the society that makes it difficult for them. But the struggle can't negate the command. Perhaps it is the struggle that will take us to *Jannah*. However, the beauty of obeying Allah remains unmatched. The reward that Muslim women will get for obeying Allah is magnificent, and we will indeed find out on the day we face Him.

If you, or someone you know is struggling with this, then encourage them, remind them of Allah's command and His mercy and help. He will not fail them. As women, we must empower and uplift each other, so we can help each other against the distress we face, thus fulfilling Allah's commands. This is how a community is formed and this is how our *Ummah* will prosper.

I knew that wearing the *Hijab* would come with challenges, but I wanted guidance. I wanted strength. I wanted to obey Allah in every way I could. All praise is to Allah, that when I was pondering these thoughts, I had beautiful role models around me who motivated me unknowingly, whom I could look up to. I thought of the mothers of the believers - the Prophet's wives, Khadijah, Asiyah, Maryam, Aisha, and his daughter Fatima (may peace be upon all them) and how they sought to obey Allah's commands despite the trying times they lived in. This became a motivation for me.

One windy August evening, during my first year of university, I made a decision. I had my diary out, and was writing some words of inspiration, as I often do, to help me relax. As I wrote, I felt a mingled rush of passion and chill. I felt a connection to my core. As I sat there, I thought to myself about what I am doing to fulfill Allah's commands. I like praying, so why don't I pray five times a day? I know wearing a *Hijab* is the right thing to do, so why can I not muster up the courage to put it on. What's stopping me?

I thought about the punishment of hell, and what it would be like. What pain would I feel? Would my bones be shattered? Would I scream at the touch of fire? I wondered about how amazing Paradise must be, where I can share a space with the Prophets (may peace be upon all of them) and have an endless amount of blessings. Everything my heart desires. It was as if hope and fear both grew in my heart rapidly with the same strength.

I knew wearing *Hijab* was an obligation on me as a Muslim woman. I also had many people remind and motivate me. I was scared because I knew people would view me differently. My own mother may not understand why I have done so, anxious about how she would answer to society, and my family members may deem me to be 'extreme' following the rhetoric of those who spurn up hate for Islam.

I watched the news, so I knew that things weren't getting easier for someone who looked like me, but I was trembling with the courage I wanted to bring forth to the world. I consciously made a decision that day to commit to wearing the *Hijab* and *Abaya* for the rest of my life. I saw this as a way for me to get closer to my Lord. I didn't want to go back because I now wanted Allah to be pleased with me. I wanted this choice to strengthen my faith, so I can continue leading a life which I will be pleased with when I face Allah.

The very next morning, I prayed my *Fajr* prayer and asked Allah to assist me. I wanted courage to face the world and the courage to answer any questions that would be thrown my way. I grabbed whatever I could find in my closet and walked out. As I walked the street to catch the bus, I had a smile on my face. I think it was this smile that repelled all the haters. I had nothing but kindness thrown at me and I didn't feel even the least bit scared. Rather, I felt comfortable and confident, untouchable and unbreakable. I knew that this would be the day I would make one of the best decisions of my life.

I guess the reason I am sharing this with you, is because I get it.

I understand that many of us are brought up in cultures that do not encourage obeying Allah. They tease us and dictate our every move. It can become overwhelmingly frustrating.

I understand that the pleasures of this world tempt and distract us. We want what we cannot have and work towards that which will only bring us to ruins, without even realizing it.

But in that ONE moment, I understood that none of it mattered if Allah is displeased. It didn't matter whether I was abiding by the norms of my culture. It did not matter whether or not I got what this world offered and met the status quo. I know this – I fear the fire of Jahannam, and I pray Allah protects us all from it, but if you want to avoid it, then you must make the conscious decision NOW. At this very moment.

Make a decision to pray, to obey Allah, to

get closer to Him. To follow His commands and become the best Muslim you can ever be.

It is ONLY He, who can help you with your efforts.

Now is the time.

Put this book down right now and call out to Him. Pray and ask Him for assistance, whatever stage you may be in your life.

Fast-forward nine years later, Allah is the only One who is getting me through. That one choice has henceforth influenced every other decision I have made. That one choice has led me to wonderful moments of success and ultimately, I have found peace in my heart knowing that I am doing what I can to obey my Lord's commands. So make a choice today and stick to it. It will change your world forever.

PLACING ALLAH FIRST

"If Allah should aid you, no one can overcome you; but if He should forsake you, who is there that can aid you after Him? And upon Allah let the believers rely."
[Quran: Soorah Aal-e-Imran, Ayah 160]

Why do we continue to rely on a world which makes us feel disempowered and lets us down? It wants us to depend on it without us realizing it is limited. We are unable to grasp that it is He who will never let us down. Were we to realize that there is benefit in both the good and the bad that happens to us, we would understand that it is He who has our best interests in mind.

I was in a grocery store once, and I have come across this type of scenario many times. I witnessed a boy who grabbed candy which bought a smile to his face and as he excitingly put it in the shopping cart, his mother gently grabbed it and put it back. This infuriated the boy and he began to throw a tantrum. I paused and thought about how mean the mother is, but immediately caught myself. When I stepped back and thought about it, I realized that this is the child's mother. She obviously loves him and cares about him more than anyone in this world. There is a wisdom behind her choice for her son, and he may not realize this now, but one day, when he's all grown and has beautiful children of his own, he will.

How many times do we feel upset about something that happens to us? We mourn, cry and complain endlessly, unable to pause and reflect on the wisdom behind it. Do we stop to consider that the overwhelming sadness is there to teach us a lesson? We forget that Allah loves us more than all His other creation, and He truly has a plan for every one of us.

We face heartache, pain, and grief. We rely on others to heal us and to fill that void in our heart. How many times have you felt sorrow in your heart, and rather than taking out a prayer mat and bowing your head in *Sujood*, you called up someone who could give you immediate comfort? This comfort is undoubtedly important, but were we to turn to Allah first, we would certainly receive a more lasting relief. We look to temporary things for lasting effects. I say this with the conviction that the only thing capable of healing us is His mercy and forgiveness. The only thing that will heal us is having a strong connection with Him.

How many times has He given you something and you thought to yourself, 'I don't deserve this', but you are still happy with what He chose for you and the blessings He bestowed.

How many times do we become arrogant over little successes and yet He still forgives us?

We are disobedient creatures of Allah, who could have easily chosen for us to be anything other than human.

But we are human.

The best of all His creations, and yet we are still ungrateful to Him. We put him last. The Prophet beautifully defined Allah's mercy so we could understand the magnitude it carried.

Abu Hurayrah (may Allah be pleased with him) narrated that the Prophet (peace be upon him) said: " Allah has one hundred parts of mercy, of which He sent down one between the Jinn, Mankind, the animals and the insects, by means of which they are compassionate and merciful to one another, and by means of which wild animals are kind to their offspring. And Allah has kept

*back ninety-nine parts of mercy with which
to be merciful to His slaves of the Day of
Resurrection" [Saheeh Muslim].*

Reflecting on this leaves me in tears because
when I remind myself of the times Allah has
shown me mercy and come to understand that
it is only one-percent, I can't be anything but
awestruck and grateful to Him.

How many of us can confidently say, that
if we died this very moment, our judgment will
be with ease? Yes, final judgment is in Allah's
hands, and if we don't live a life according to
His will and do the things that make Him happy,
we will regret every moment we breathed on
this earth. We have no excuses to disobey Him.
None. So ask yourself what you can do today to
rekindle your relationship with Allah.

It is as if over time, we become blind. We
become slaves of this world when we should
only be slaves to the Merciful Creator. We
forget that it is He who allowed us to enter this
world and it is He who allows us to breathe
and showers His infinite blessings upon us. It
is He who has perfectly designed this world and
everything in it.

Pause and ask yourself, what is preventing

you from building that relationship with Allah? What is stopping you from getting closer to Him? What is stopping you from worshipping Him and obeying His commands?

Will you wait until your last breath? If you're still breathing, then it's not too late.

HER CONVICTION IN ALLAH

Allah is so amazing. His capabilities are unmatched by those of humankind. His ability to set certain trials and paths for us, knowing this is what will benefit us, amazes me. He is perfect and His plan is perfect. This is something we must seek to understand so we can come to terms with everything that happens in our lives. People who enter our lives and cross our paths are there for a reason. They are meant to be there and change our lives forever. They are there so we can learn from them and grow through them, and I do believe that even one person can have a lasting impact on you.

In 2017, Allah brought a beautiful *Muslimah* into my life.

I watched her for several months as she inspired people across the globe through her words and her commitment. I stumbled across her story in which she spoke about the trials she has faced. They inspired me because I saw a resemblance of many women I have met in my life. She inspired me because of the courage and resilience she was facing her life with. She made me feel comfortable before I even entered into a conversation with her. I felt attracted to her because I was touched by her. Her story. Her zeal. Her sincerity in serving others.

She is a strong and fierce woman. A change-maker, to say the least.

After struggling with some personal limitations that came up when I was serving other people, I reached out to her with the hope that perhaps she could guide me to be as great as she is. I asked her some coaching questions and immediately, from the second she responded, she began assisting me. She asked me if we can get on a video call and I agreed, not knowing the impact it would leave on me. We had a lengthy and constructive conversation which then led us to this very gripping interaction.

She asked me to close my eyes and imagine the life I wanted in the following year. I did so very gently and got in a comfortable position so that I may reflect and connect with my deepest thoughts. I peeked an eye open and surely, she was doing the exercise with me. As I opened my eyes I felt excited and overwhelmed. She leaned in, and although there was a computer screen between us, it almost felt like she was going to come right out and give me a hug.

Her expressions showed me that she gets it. She wants me to have what I want.

At that moment, I thought to myself, "I should be happy. I've met a wonderful person. She's nice. She's friendly. We joked. We laughed. We exchanged good thoughts. Everything we spoke about has been positive. I should be pleased. So why am I sad?"

I suddenly realized what was wrong. It had nothing to do with our meeting. It was deep down, inside me, somehow suppressed for years. I became overwhelmed with tears because I knew what I wanted, but I didn't believe it was possible. I wanted it so badly and the intensity of my desire scared me. She watched me cry. She watched me shake. She allowed me to experience what I was experiencing because she knew this was the only way I would grow.

I expressed to her the very thing I didn't want to utter from my mouth, because I was scared it may show disbelief in Allah, "I don't know," I shook my head, "I don't think I can do it."

She did not respond immediately, and I remember her silence to this day.

She sat there for a long while, and then with conviction, she asked me, "Why not?"

34

Startled at her blatancy, I wasn't sure how to respond. It was a simple question but for some reason, I was speechless. I didn't know the answer. All I could muster was a feeble, "I'm not sure."

She then reminded me, with deep sentiments that, "Nothing is impossible for Allah." She said that it is WE who misunderstand Him and live with the belief that He is limited when indeed He is not. He is capable of ALL things. She had so much determination in her voice that it made me feel guilty. How could I doubt Allah's ability? I felt ashamed, but I knew, at that moment, a shift had taken place, one that would reaffirm my belief in Allah and change my life forever.

Even today, whenever I feel hopeless, whenever I feel sad and forlorn, down and depressed, I am reminded of her words and they give me comfort and courage.

Nothing is impossible for Allah. He is capable of much more than we can comprehend. If we came to terms with this reality, we could work towards creating the life we desire. Our Duas would become more powerful. We wouldn't hesitate to ask, rather we would go to Him for all of our hearts' desires. I am certain that knowing and living this reality will change your life forever.

Remember this, my beautiful sisters. Nothing is impossible for Allah.

"When He decrees a thing. He only says to it 'BE' and it is"

[Quran: Soorah Maryam Ayah 35]

ON THE JOURNEY OF BEING YOU

On the journey of being you, you must know that Allah comes first. You will never reach your full potential without the assistance of Allah. You will falter in your efforts of being your best-self when your heart is void of Allah. So to be your best self, you have to give importance to the Best.

REFLECTION QUESTIONS

1. Am I living a life that Allah is pleased with?

2. What actions can I take to fix my relationship with Allah?

3. Where does the importance of Allah and His commands fall in my life?

4. What does Islam mean to me?

EXERCISE

EVALUATING MY CONNECTION WITH ALLAH

This exercise is very basic, but incredibly powerful.

Do it with honesty and it can change your life.

1. On a piece of paper, write down: Prayers, Quran, some of the obligations to Allah i.e *Hijab*, Remembrance of Allah.

2. Rank each of them from 1-10 based on how well you feel you are following them, or how consistent you are.

This will give you a visualization of which areas you need to improve and work on.

Now that you have made a conscious decision, think about one or two actions that you can do to improve each area.

Realize this- No one can help you if you do not help yourself. The first step is yours, and only yours to take. You have to make the effort and push yourself. *Shaytaan* will do everything in his ability to bog you down. To stall you and steer you in another direction. You have to fight it with all your inner and outer strength. The battle will be long and difficult, but its bounty will be forever sweet and fruitful.

Your journey starts today.

You are not alone, so reach out to me and let's see how we can support each other.

You got this!

Two years ago, I returned to my family a shattered and battered woman, a mother of two children and pregnant with a third. The worst part of this was that my soul was almost non-existent, and my connection with Allah the Almighty was almost non-existent. I had so much pain and resentment. I couldn't understand why my relationship with Allah was so weak. There were so many underlying factors that contributed to this. Alhamdulillah, after working with Kulsoom, I began healing, placing my trust and reliance on Allah. 'You just need hard work and patience' she would always say

'trust in the process' and I learned that trusting the process was also trusting Allah's decree.

— Maryam Hussein, United Kingdom

I remember a Ramadan when I was at my lowest in life and spirituality. I began listening to lectures by Islamic Scholars, and slowly the belief grew within me that Allah is truly capable of everything. I devoted time to prayer and supplication, and it was miraculous how quickly my perspective of things changed. I learned that it was truly about trusting His Perfection, and knowing that you are exactly where you need to be. When you remember His magnitude, you remember that He is capable of all things. Nothing is too big or too small for Him. This understanding has changed how I view life. No matter the problem, I know that trusting Allah (Subhanahu-Wa-Ta'ala) is the first step. This does not negate the effort you need to put into your life, but it does reassure you that Allah (Subhanahu-Wa-Ta'ala) is always there for you.

— Banan Alawi, Canada

Worship Allah. He's all that you really have. Love for Him will get you through everything. This world will not.

VISION

Whatever your passion, now is the time to pursue it

HER DETERMINATION

I have always, and forever shall, been inspired by the people I meet. They give me a sense of belonging to this world. A world which I resented for long. I find such people to be kind and inspirational, to say the least, but wrapped up in conflict.

This conflict manifests within them into chaos, and yet I still see their inner beauty. It is my deepest belief that amidst the chaos, people rise, and it is in this rising that my soul finds peace.

This isn't just a story. This was a realization. This was the moment that would perhaps stay with me forever because it gave me confidence in the very thing I aim to live for - service. It is people like her who urge me to leave my comfortable bed every morning and take measures to make a difference in this world.

I remember this day vividly for the motivation it gave me. On that day, I roamed around the home anxious to make a change. My cat continued her usual routine of sleep, eat, play, and demand attention. Her presence usually gives me comfort. However, I do not recall giving her much attention that day. I had only just begun my venture some six months before. I had made many connections and a fair share of beautiful relationships. Yet, I still longed for something more. I wanted to make more change. I wanted to impact people on a larger scale. Have you ever started something and wanted to make it bigger and better because you know the project has potential? You know it'll be worth it in the end so you want to spend every ounce of energy you have on it? That is precisely how I felt.

My husband usually calls me from work and that day he asked me, "How is your day going?"

I replied, "It's okay."

He did not probe me even though he knew something was wrong. I had been in a state of unease for several weeks. I wanted to kick start 2018 by forming more relationships and I was antsy because I was yet to meet someone who made me believe in my work and remind me of the very reason I do what I do. As I was lying down in bed, scrolling through my social media accounts, I came across a message that made me jump up.

Part of it read, "...this New Year I would love to do a session with you on personal coaching."

I felt a tingle of excitement run through my whole body. I wanted to help her and make a difference in her life, so I quickly responded with my number. A few hours later we got on a call. I asked her to tell me about herself, and to date, I am still in awe of the things she has experienced in her life and the bravery she has faced them with. Imagine my surprise when I was reminded that we went to University together. I proceeded further with our conversation and asked her why she wanted to work with me and what she wanted to achieve in the following year.

She paused and took a deep breath, and with the utmost confidence, she told me everything she wanted to accomplish. She wanted to start and run her own business. She wanted to marry and settle down. She wanted to increase her *Imaan* and attain a better relationship with Allah.

I listened intently, resonating with her every ambition and excitement. I too have felt the same ambition before, have had the same excitement about my dreams and goals. I told her, "I would love to work with you and support you."

Determined, we both agreed to commit to a working relationship, in which I would help her dreams come true, and be her cheerleader throughout the journey. After we discussed minute details, we finished up the call, and I sat there in silence. I was inspired.

To this date, she is one of the most precious relationships I have ever formed. I asked myself 'What is so special about her?'

My cat, Lily, curled up by my side while I pondered in silence. The state I was in – pure bliss. The thoughts of working with her excited me. They made me eager to start out work right away and to help her become the best version of herself that she has ever seen.

After a long moment of deep thought, I realized that yes, she had determination in her voice. Yes, she wanted support, but most importantly she knew the life that she wanted to create. She had been through so many trials, but she was determined to make a change in her life. This is what amazed me. Ever since we formed that relationship, she has been dedicated to her dreams. I admired her courage to face her truths. I adored her ability to be raw.

I wondered for many months why I enjoyed working with her and what made her stand out.

I can now say that it was her VISION.

She knew what she wanted, and the want was so powerful that it didn't matter what I had said on that call or what the terms of our agreement were. She didn't give much importance to the fear she felt of how uncomfortable our sessions may get. She knew what she wanted, and *Alhamdulillah*, she is achieving so much more than that. The vision was bigger than herself and this is what made her take action every single day.

Having a clear vision can enable you to take all sorts of 'leaps of faith', and that's what she is doing every day - facing her fears head on and making her dreams come true.

I'm grateful because I get to watch her every step of the way and celebrate her wins.

Let us not forget that the Prophet (peace be upon him) lived a life which required him to take a lot of calculated risks and important steps so that the message of Islam can spread and flourish. He rose up against polytheists with determination and a strong will. This required a clear vision and an immense amount of perseverance and ambition. One such example that outlined his vision and guided his steps was his migration from Makkah to

Madinah. It was very carefully planned. Each step and its setbacks taken into consideration. He kept his goal of reaching Madinah in mind and this motivated him to move forward with perseverance and hence the steps that he took to achieve that goal was successful because he sought the assistance of Allah and made a proper plan.

THE IMPORTANCE OF VISION

I have always been a reflective one, often times been ridiculed because of it. However, I have never felt ashamed of my ability to reflect on the world around me and my ability to learn from my own life experiences. I have, since I was a young girl, observed the people around me. I noticed that some were very ambitious and were accomplishing great things in their life. I also noticed that there were some who were struggling in their endeavors and lacked motivation. Oh boy, did they have it tough, because society would always tend to put them down. They were bright and brilliant people, but there was something missing, distinguishing them from the others.

I created two categories for the people in the world. There are the people fighting every day to make their dreams come true. They are let down by society, but they get up and work harder. On the other hand, there are those who are unsure of what they want in life, but they have the potential. They have the zeal, and once they commit and have a vision, they go at it full force. However, it's the commitment and vision that is hindering.

I believe everyone has so much potential and so much awesomeness that they can put out to the world. Through the people I have met and the experiences I have had, I know that people are generally goal-oriented. They want things. They yearn for things. Often enough they work for things. However, amidst all this wanting and yearning, we limit ourselves, our abilities, and our actions. We limit ourselves from growth. We stop our beautiful side from emerging and blossoming.

In this process, we misunderstand Allah's abilities and because of the limitations we put on ourselves, we fail to understand everything Allah is capable of. Have you ever looked at the branch of a tree and thought to yourself how is it possible for it to be so complex and so beautiful. It is possible. Allah is capable of that and much more. The Almighty who created the world around us, breathed a soul into us, paves out our life. He forgives us when we err and cry out of fear. He accepts our *Duas* - the ones we cry for till our eyes are numb. He is so merciful to us every step of the way, yet again we misunderstand Him and live off the belief that He is not capable of making certain things happen when indeed He is. We fail to aim high because we simply don't think He is capable enough to give it to us. We stop dreaming because we think perhaps it may never come true. I assure you with every breath I have, that He will. He will make your dreams come true. He will give us what we ask for and work for. More than often, something even better. All we have do is ask. All we have to do is try. All we need is to put our faith and devotion to Him and understand Him.

It's like the example of the bird who goes out empty handed and when he returns to his nest in the evening, his stomach is full. How blessed is he that he has a Lord above him watching over His affairs?

Allah says in the Qur'an;
'And when my slaves ask you (O Muhammad) concerning Me, then (answer them), I am indeed near (to them by knowledge). I respond to the invocations of the supplicant when he calls on Me (without any mediator or intercessor). So let them obey Me and believe in Me, so that they may be led aright'
[Sooratul Baqarah, 2: 186]

Deep down, we know what we want, but we are scared of asking Allah out of the uncertainty of our *Dua* being accepted. We become ignorant of Allah's abilities and this turns us away from asking from Him. We know what we want, yet we fail to put it into words and actions.

It's okay. It happened to me as well. I didn't think my dreams were worth discussing. Have you ever spoken to that child who has dreams so big that their eyes brighten up when they're telling you? That feeling is great. It has hope in it. When that feeling goes away, one is left with despair.

I remember telling my husband one day, "Maybe I am not good enough. Why would Allah give me all these things? I don't deserve this and even if I got it, I don't think I could handle it."

Have you ever uttered something like this or held such beliefs?

Do you see how I limited my abilities? My ability to create the life I desire and work towards it. Do you see how I misunderstood Allah's abilities? His ability to give us the life we yearn for. I always wanted great things, but I thought I was meant to live an ordinary life.

I thought I couldn't have things that I dreamed of. Through my teenage years and into my early adulthood, I lived life like this until I realized that if I were to just muster up a little hope, perhaps things would be different. If I were to just clear up my vision and work towards it, I could really change the world. If I simply bow down, put my hands up and ask Allah, I could be among those who have it all, and be content with it. If I made some goals and charged at them, full-speed, I could really do amazing things. My limitations were stopping me.

Lasting success doesn't come by chance. It comes by taking a clear path and reminding yourself why you want that thing. What makes you cringe when you think about the life you don't want? What makes you excited when you tell someone the life you have always imagined? It comes by asking Allah because when you ask, He gives. When you work for it, believe that great things will be achieved.

You have to want it so badly that when you get up in the morning, you're excited and eager.

Knowing what you want will guide you to the right people, right places, and right *Duas*. It's almost as if the universe will alter itself just to help you achieve your dreams and bring

your vision to life. As Muslims, we should aim
to do extraordinary things and for this, we need
a vision.

RENEWING YOUR VISION

Life happens.

We lose track.

That's normal.

I have had many moments in the past when I was unable to get out of bed. There were times in my life when I was overwhelmed by grief. I lacked motivation and my body couldn't move. I seemed like I had it all together and to some extent I did, but there was something clouding my mind and heart. I was making attempts to fix my relationship with Allah, which was the only thing that kept me going. But I no longer felt the same. I felt dark clouds above me. I was losing hope in myself. I had goals. I have always been ambitious, but I wasn't working towards them. My laziness was getting the best of me and my attitude suffered as a result.

How many times do we struggle with our every limb to get out of bed in the morning for the very thing we were once excited about? That feeling of over-joy that came with the goals we set out so passionately. It's as if that feeling has been stolen from us. It's as if that joy is lost.

I recall an experience that I had with an acquaintance whom I always knew to be upbeat and ambitious. She was zealous in her actions and had goals she was actively working on. Some few months later I bumped into her in the hallway of our University and she seemed very down. Her posture had changed and her face seemed pale. I approached her out of curiosity.

"Hey, how are you?" I told her that I often saw her in the halls and events and she always seemed very sure of what she wants which is why I couldn't help but approach her when I saw quite the opposite. "Would you like to chat?" I urged her.

She responded, "Yes, I would very much like that."

We barely sat down and tears trembled down her face.

"I feel like my whole world is falling apart," she lifted her face out of her palms. "My husband and I have gone through a divorce and I'm not quite sure I know how to carry my life forward."

I was completely shocked, but with an empathetic voice, I urged her on. "What is it that you want in life?"

She said, "I want to be happy. I want to be like I was before."

"Then what is stopping you?"

She paused hesitantly, stared at me, and with more tears she said, "Me. I am stopping me."

As soon as she said it, she smiled and it's as if this burden was suddenly off her shoulders. This heavy weight she was carrying around.

In that moment, all I had to do was reassure her that she had the abilities. She has what it takes to work towards her goals. Yes, this trial has put a pause on her endeavors, but that doesn't mean she can't return to it stronger than ever.

And she did.

We touched base a few years later and she had applied to law school, traveled to two countries and was re-approaching marriage with a new perspective.

We get so busy in the hustle and bustle of life, that we forget our vision, what really matters. We allow our trials to dwell in our hearts which cloud our ability to take positive actions forward. We occupy ourselves with lavish things because they give us a temporary satisfaction. We surround ourselves with outcomes which only stay with us as long as a bird keeps its prey.

Today. Today is when you must stop and connect with your soul, your core. It is this moment, when you feel lost, that you must make the effort to be found.

As Muslims, we must always renew our intentions, but with our intentions, we must renew our vision.

Ask yourself - what is it that I really want and where do I want to go?

Reflections like these will connect you back to what you are meant to do in this world. They will connect you back to the very thing that gets you overjoyed and eager.

For if your vision wasn't lost, how would your purpose ever be re-found...stronger and better?

The world needs more of you, so clear up your vision and embark on a journey where you can change the world. Where you can make a difference. Imagine a world with more of these people. Truly, we would be a force unstoppable.

VISION AS A MUSLIM

'And We have not created the heaven and earth and what is between them in vain. That is the opinion of those who disbelieve'
[Qur'an: 38: 27]

As Muslims, we are meant to be purposeful individuals. Allah sent us to this world with the purpose of worshiping and obeying His every command. Our purpose is to spread the message of Islam until we are returned to Allah and perhaps even leave our legacy on this earth. Our mission in this world is to revive this *Ummah*, to bring it back to that peaceful cohesive state we once lived in, or the state we are meant to live in. Keeping this in mind, our vision should be extraordinary.

We must strive, with every bone in our body, to do something for the *Ummah* that will lead it to its destiny. We must be amongst those who get up every day and fight the good fight, who speak up against injustices. We must have a vision where we see people helping each other and not destroying each other. A vision of living in a world where a little girl can run around the street and not be worried about misconduct. A world where individuals do not have to dismay about the injustices they face. A just society. A vision where we are abiding by the laws of Allah and not of the limited man.

A mighty vision like this requires those who are truly vision oriented. We cannot, at a time like this, sit in our homes and watch others do the work. We cannot pass our burdens to our sons and our daughters. We have to stand up, do that work and set that example. We have to be amongst those who bring this *Ummah* back to its promised state. So as a Muslim, having a vision becomes truly important. Something we must master before our breath is taken away. If not now, never. If not today, when?

In order to achieve this, we must also remind ourselves of the words of Prophet Muhammad (peace be upon him) where he said: *"No one of you becomes a true believer until he likes for his brother what he likes for himself."* (Bukhari)

I want to dedicate the following words to one of my teachers, Shaykh Mohammad Osta, who taught me to live for a purpose greater than myself.

I observed him for many years and every time I see him. He has passion in his eyes and his words. His tears are an attestation to his tender heart which aches at the pains of the *Ummah*. I questioned myself many times as to why I cannot have this same passion and zeal. I admired him and his ability to shake hearts of those he spoke to, by simply stating the truth. He lives a vision once lived by our beloved Prophet (may peace and blessings be upon him). So what could be nobler than that? May Allah bless him and guide him in his endeavors and sacrifices for this *Ummah*. May we all follow the footsteps of our beloved Prophet and revive this *Ummah*.

Know this. Your vision means nothing if it is not in line with what Allah wants from you. You will be at a terrible loss on the day you stand in front of Him, if all you focused on was yourself and forgot the *Ummah*. So have a vision, but let it be greater than yourself. Have a vision where working on yourself is only a means to the end goal. Have a vision which benefits that goal for the sake of benefiting the greater good. This *Ummah* needs us. It needs you. And your extraordinary vision is what will guide you.

ON THE JOURNEY OF BEING YOU

On the journey of being you, you have to have a clear vision. Know what you want. Know what you need and know how you are going to get there. Without a vision, you are like a bird without a head. Only when you accomplish what you are meant to be will you be the best version of yourself.

REFLECTION QUESTIONS

1. Where do I see myself in the following year? Next two years? Next five years?

2. What is it that will excite me enough to get out of bed every morning?

3. What does Allah want from me and how can I work towards it?

4. How can I give back to the *Ummah*?

EXERCISE

CREATING A VISION BOARD

This is a very exciting exercise if you are like me - a visual person. You will enjoy it, and even if you are not a visual person, this exercise will definitely motivate you.

1. This step requires you to get a board or paper. Get creative!

2. Visualize your ambitions. Cut up pictures of everything you have ever dreamed about and want in life: That fancy car, that wonderful job, that amazing opportunity, money, anything and everything! Glue it to the board in any manner you wish.

3. Place it where you can see it every day. On the fridge, in your office or workspace. This will remind you of what you want every single day and motivate you to work towards that thing.

Now, you can make *Dua* for each thing and begin to take the steps necessary to make it come true. The more consistent you are, the closer you will levitate towards your goals and ambitions.

May Allah allow you to achieve your goals and bring your vision to reality.

Ameen

"Working with Kulsoom helped me understand that my values, my goals and my vision are all interconnected. Having a vision in life has helped me work towards living a purposeful life. It led me to rediscover my passion and strengths and how to use them to achieve all I wanted in life."

Marjaan Alam, Canada

"Kulsoom helped me discover the opportunity to think deeply about what my goals were, why I wanted to achieve them and the steps I needed to take to get there. I spent time thinking about

what my vision in life was and how I could create goals that aligned with this vision. Having a vision is extremely important as it allows you to focus on the bigger picture. Many goals can be difficult for us to achieve, but we know that our lives will be better once we have achieved them. Having a larger vision serves as motivation when you are struggling to achieve your goals.

I have spent time creating multiple vision boards. These vision boards have images of the things I want to achieve in my life. When I see these images, I get excited and this pushes me forward. I have also crafted dream duas for each of the images on my vision board. This is where I attach a specific name of Allah to my Dua. So whenever I am struggling with achieving my goals, I stop to think about my vision and I spend time saying my dream Duas. I believe that incorporating your vision with action and Duas is a powerful combination for true change in your life"

— Amirah Zaky, United Kingdom

Create a vision so big that it becomes your reason to get up every morning

RELATIONSHIPS

True success lies in support of one another

MY DIVORCE SHAPED ME

At some point in life, we all face trials filled with heartaches and pain. We all have those moments when we are overwhelmed by grief. In those moments we experience darkness and anxiety like a ship lost at sea in the midst of a storm. We all experience things beyond our thoughts and abilities. They push us to our limits and we find ourselves desperately praying to Allah because in those moments we are in need of Him. It is through these heart churning trials that we are able to learn a lesson and grow.

My life has been a series of such magnificent lessons. Each chapter in my book has taught me to rely on Allah. It forced me to the ground so I could weep in prayer, for I know only Allah will help me through. It has taught me about the essence of life. That pain is inevitable and it forces us to turn to God. Without it, we take things for granted. It has taught me to feel every emotion I go through.

As we go through life and connect with ourselves, and those around us, we make choices. Some choices make us proud, and some choices leave us at the doorstep of pain, but nevertheless wrapped in a lesson. I can confidently and happily say, that through each choice I made and trials that I have endured, I learned something valuable. I have grown from them and these lessons are what make me, 'me'. It is what I offer to my clients, my loved ones and the world.

If we can't grow from our trials and learn from them, then truly we are failing this test of life. These lessons are helping us prepare for our meeting with our Lord and these trials are quizzes we must ace. If we fail, we try again, but we must never give up. For in giving up is where we lose ourselves.

Ponder on your life and the trials you faced. Think about the lessons you learned. I assure you, those are your strengths.

As I approached the age of 20, Allah bestowed upon me the gift of marriage. He allowed me to be a part of what is supposed to be a beautiful and sacred, life-long bond. He allowed me to connect with someone who was supposed to be my best friend, my partner, in all to come.

It was a long-distance marriage which was unfortunately short-lived. One that ended in eight short months. I didn't experience what I thought I would. Bliss, unconditional love, respect, admiration, communication. I didn't get the reassurance I needed or the emotional support I yearned for all my life. Love wasn't unconditional, and this I realized after I got married.

As I share my story with the world, I remind myself of the realization I re-lived every day after my divorce - That I got married for the wrong reasons. I share these reasons because I find many women also getting married for similar reasons and facing the pain of broken marriages. For one, I fell into the pressures of society. I understood love in an artificial way and not what it should be understood and expressed as.

Love is beautiful. Love is accepting the other person for who they are and growing together. Love is about both halves making balanced compromises for each other. Love is patience and gratitude. Love is a feeling that grows in your heart every day you are married. As I study the life of our beloved Prophet (peace be upon him), I am reminded of how he exhibited love in his relationships specifically with his spouses.

A'isha (may Allah be pleased with her) reported that the Messenger of Allah would give her a vessel to drink, when she was menstruating, then he would look for the spot where she had put her lips on and put his lips on the same spot. [An-Nasai, authenticated by Albani]

This is proof for me that love is beautiful and necessary for a relationship to bloom. Love is not all about material gifts and romance.

But I? I grew up admiring fairy tales where the prince is head over heels for the princess. I was attracted to the notion where a man is sophisticated and mysterious. I developed an unhealthy attachment and waited for love all my life. I relied on others to meet my emotional needs. Love for me became about romantic words and gestures that I saw in the media. It became about expecting gifts as a sign of true love. Love became something I yearned for, and although I had lots of love to give, I spent more time searching for someone who could love me rather than if he was deserving of my love.

I now realize that one can have an amazing marriage. A man can love a woman deeply. A woman's emotions are important. I realize this now because I am married to a man who understands the virtue of a woman and the sanctity of marriage. He deserves my love and our bond is more than material things and romantic gestures. It's about acceptance, compromise, understanding, growth, and communication. All of which I lacked when I was drowning in a nonsensical notion of what made up a marriage.

I wasn't satisfied with my first marriage, because I married him for what I thought he was, not who he was. I was blinded by my fantasy and unable to realize what could make or break a marriage. I understand that everyone is on their own journey, and perhaps he too needed to heal and grow, but that bond wasn't one we could continue having committed to a relationship. Communication failed on both our parts. Love seemed like a battle ground. Emotions didn't seem to be of importance and I was withering away. Sometimes two people must grow outside of a relationship, outside of a commitment, separately in their own way. This is how they will flourish and bloom like a rose. *Alhamdulillah*, Allah saved me because I never lived with this man, but the lessons I learned in those eight agonizing months were so profound.

Throughout those eight months, I kept asking Allah,

"Why am I facing this pain?"

"Why am I always crying?" and,

"Why don't I feel happy?"

I begged for answers. I yearned for clarity. I spent countless restless nights in agony and sorrow.

I realized that these feelings were a mercy from Allah. I needed to feel and experience them, so I can grow. I needed to live them, so I can pave my way out of them. I needed to learn from my choices, so the next time I am married, I can make a better choice for a husband. And perhaps, through my journey, I can help those who have made the same choices I did.

Signing the *Khulu'u* (divorce) papers was one of the hardest things I have done in my life. I remember sitting on the floor for several hours, unable to move. I was unable to fathom the concept of signing out of such a relationship. I had trouble letting go.

All my life, I had thought that relationships were meant to be forever, but forever is fictitious because forever isn't for anyone. Eternity is for Allah. We are living in a bubble of temporary time, which will pop. Therefore, to expect that any relationship will last forever, that you'll be able to hold on to someone forever, is wrong. It will leave you sourly disappointed.

This experience taught me a lesson.

See, we all experience emotional pain. It is how you grow from it that stays with you forever. It taught me that not all relationships are meant to last. Sometimes it is to our benefit that we let them go. Some relationships are meant to be adored from far away and some are cherished up close. Some people are simply not meant to be a part of your life. And it is in this lesson that I grew.

I set boundaries. I understood who to let in my life and who to keep at the tip. I understood who was beneficial for my growth and who was detrimental. I learned who to let in my life and who to keep away. I chose my friends carefully. Most importantly, I learned how to let go, a concept I struggled with since I was young.

Alhamdulillah, I am now happily married to the man of my dreams and it was because of my trial, experience, and journey, that this was possible.

So I pray, that through my story, I have

touched your heart and that you have come to the realization that the choices you make, matter. Who you keep in your life, matters. Who you let go, matters. These choices may break you temporarily, but they will shape you permanently.

All relationships are an important and integral part of who you are. You must choose them wisely and accept those that aren't meant to be.

I pray that you learn from my lessons and from your own.

Don't forget to try the exercise in the end.

ATTACHMENTS

We each have a heart which is soft and yearning to give love. We all have such encounters.

I recall my one of many encounters with a newborn baby. A beautiful girl. So soft in her composure. When you look at her, you feel calmness and joy. The way she looks at you with her eyes. You can see the innocence and purity. When she reaches out, you know that she has nothing but love to give and wants nothing but love in return. I find most people to be not so different in their desire to give and receive love. We are all born with a soft heart, thirsting for this love. However, on this path, we attach ourselves to many things- people, concepts, ideas, and material things. We believe this will fill that void inside us.

We believe that we will get back the same energy we give to others. We believe it will make us whole. We spend all our energy on people who don't matter and run away from those who do.

How many times has this happened, and you realize that something is wrong?

That energy sometimes doesn't come back. That love sometimes isn't reciprocated and that void, more than often, cannot be filled. In the end, no one but you is hurt.

I have been down this path many times, especially in my first marriage.

The thing to realize is this; when you love someone, you build an attachment. You grow fonder of them and your bond strengthens. It is natural. Unavoidable.

Let us not forget the tears in the eyes of our beloved Prophet and his saddened heart at the loss of his wife Khadija (may Allah be pleased with her).

However, when there are two imperfect beings in a relationship, conflict is bound to happen. This is also unavoidable. That person may say or do something which can leave you devastated, because our actions are not meant to be perfect. We are not meant to be perfect. The realization then lies in the fact that because human beings are imperfect, we ought not to distress ourselves when we are hurt. We ought not to expect that we will not be hurt. It is bound to happen. It is in this false expectation, thinking that it won't happen, where we fail to understand our hurt because we are too preoccupied with thoughts like, 'Why did it happen?'

But with Allah, it is beautifully different. He is perfect, far beyond what you can imagine. Were our hearts to attach to Allah, and were we to truly understand that every single thing He has destined for us is good for us, we would be able to understand our pain. We would still feel pain. We would still feel hurt and experience sorrow, but we would understand that there is a reason we are going through what we go through. Allah wouldn't put us in this position if we weren't capable of going through it. Conflict is imminent between humankind, and a result of this conflict is the hurt, pain, and sorrow we feel.

However, when we feel hurt because of something Allah chose for us, there is beauty in it because Allah's plan is perfect for us. Allah wants best for all His servants. Were our hearts preoccupied with Allah, and were we to understand His true essence, we would be able to reason with our pain.

Love your husband, your parents, your children, relatives, and friends, but anything that interferes in your eternal love for Allah is nothing but torture unto yourself. A bittersweet poison.

We have to learn how to set boundaries and govern who to let in. This will save us from the heartaches of broken relationships. See, a good relationship helps you connect to your core and when you connect to your core, you are making space for the love of Allah. However, if you don't let go of those toxic and hurtful relationships, how will there ever be space for what really matters, who really matters? If you set false expectations about others, and about Allah, how will you ever understand your pain?

Attach yourself to Allah, and I promise that He will never let you down. This will reflect in your relationship with Him and with other people.

This realization is needed to successfully get through life.

RELATIONSHIPS

"O mankind, fear your Lord, who created
you from one soul and created from it its
mate and dispersed from both of them many
men and women. And fear Allah, through
whom you ask one another, and (do not cut
the relations of) the wombs. Indeed Allah
is ever, over you, an Observer"

[Qur'an: Soorah An-Nisa, Ayah 1]

Our parents. The first relationship we are
born into. Our siblings, our relatives, the
loved ones all around us waiting to befriend us
from the moment of our birth. We form more
relationships as we go through life. One cannot
escape relationships even after death. They are
there when we are being buried, and they cry
for us after we have departed. They make Dua
for us even after we have gone.

I have seen and witnessed the isolation
individuals feel when they don't know people.
They are living by themselves with barely
anyone around them. They hardly meet people
or form new connections. For some, it is hard
to keep even one relationship, because they fail

to understand what makes relationships work, and others are longing for more because they realize these are what will help them grow.

That's life. We run from one relationship to another. On one mount we strengthen a tie and on another, we are hurt. As we grow and prosper, so do our relationships. The ones that break are a sign that they are not meant to stay with us forever.

It is very important to build our relationships. We cannot escape them, so we might as well nurture them. Give them the time and respect they deserve. Put in the efforts that are necessary to make them last. These relationships help us. We learn from them and grow from them. They are the ones who will be at your funeral and pray for your wellbeing even in the Hereafter.

It's true, that one day no relation will matter. The Day of Judgment. When we will be trembling with fear. Our lives will flash before our eyes. We will be so preoccupied with what we did and didn't do, and no relationship will come and rescue us because they will be worried about themselves. However, while we are in this Dunya, we have to assist and support each other, because we will be questioned about those relationships. We will have to atone for those we hurt, and those who hurt as a consequence of our misdemeanors. We have to be kind and generous with each other. Uplift each other.

I believe that we are all on the same boat in this life, so why not be there for each other?

If it wasn't for the people around me (you know who you are!), I may not have been able to get through the trials I have faced. Thus, I say with confidence, that support makes a huge difference. Be that support.

I have accounted for two important relationships in my life. I believe these relationships are vital for one to have and cherish.

MY BEST FRIEND

After I finished high school, one could say I lost many friends. I changed. My priorities changed. I still loved my friends, but we all went our separate ways. I remember making *Dua* to Allah, pleading, "O Allah please grant me a companion who will stand by me in hardships and in joy. One who will support me and I will support her." I stressed this *Dua* for many days to come, continuously reminiscing the relationship Prophet Muhammad had with his companion and best friend, Abu Bakr As-Siddiq (may Allah be pleased with them both).

It was important for me to have a companion in the form of a friend who I could enjoy my time with. Someone I could share my life with. Then I had this encounter.

I graduated from University where I served as VP for the MSA (Muslim Students Association). We were planning a bake sale, which I was leading, and one of my tasks involved compiling a list of people who could contribute to the event.

I was really stressed out, as there was so much to do, so much to sort out. I was alone in the room, or so I thought I was, fidgeting with my pen and notepad, crossing out items on my list, replacing them with newer ones. I sighed with frustration at my chicken-scratch scribblings, utterly distraught, when I heard someone behind me.

"Are you okay?" She stepped into the room, a touch of eagerness in her voice.

"I'm fine," I responded with a reserved attitude. It was not that I intentionally wanted to be closed-off, but the growing mountain of work and a closely approaching deadline of the bake sale was really driving me to an edge.

Somehow, she did not seem to get the hint.

"Would you like some help?" She asked persistently.

I sighed with obvious irritation and decided to test her resilience. I explained what I was working on and the problem I was having. I needed contributors to the bake sale, and was having trouble finding any.

She immediately volunteered to contribute, and somehow, in a flash, all my worries seemed to dissipate.

The following day, she came to me, distressed and agitated, declaring that she had burnt all the cookies she had baked for the event.

Another setback.

Another hitch.

Another level of stress for me.

The irritation I had when she first approached me, rushed back into me with fire. I held myself with an immense muster over my emotions. All things considered, I had a choice.

She had made a mistake. She was sincere about it. I chose to forgive.

I am not quite sure how our friendship grew after that. We shared so many moments similar to these, and even more moments with deep sentiments. We have now become important parts of each other's lives. We have carried each other through tears and laughter.

She is my life.

A special part of my heart.

If you have a good friend, a friend close to your heart, then you will understand and feel what I feel.

A best friend is a relationship you must cherish forever. She was my *Dua* come true, a gift in disguise. I pray Allah blesses everyone with such a gift.

A best friend isn't like any other relationship; just as any other relationship isn't like friendship. Every relationship has boundaries, limits, tolerances, and a friendship has its equal share, only unique. You can be yourself. You can laugh and cry at the same time. There are things you can tell your best friend which you cannot share even with your spouse, your parents, your siblings, or anyone else in this world.

Therefore, if you have a best friend, I urge you to keep them close. If you don't then ask Allah, because a best friend is your partner through thick and thin.

MY COACH

This relationship is special to me, because this person taught me how to be the best version of myself and become a better coach every day.

After I started my journey as a life coach, I soon realized the importance of having someone there for you, who would go deeper and help you achieve your personal goals. I began to understand the heavy weight I carry on my shoulders when speaking to people about their personal lives, thus there needed to be someone who would help me ease that burden. Someone who would point out my own mistakes and limiting beliefs, and assist me so that through that example and energy, I may assist others.

I went through a tiring journey of finding a coach who was suitable for me until this individual reached out and offered a helping hand I was oblivious to. One day, however, I decided to send him a message and express my gratitude and my slight frustration of being unable to find a coach who I could work with. I remember our first conversation when I had spilled my heart out about my desires to make a change and wanted to work with someone who was sincere and helpful. I didn't know what service meant until I started working with my coach. At first, I was hesitant because I didn't know this person, but I realized that the capacity to serve and to help others see things from a different perspective, was untouchable. This coach had something that others did not – a beautiful heart and the desire to create relationships. Everyone needs someone in their life who helps them become better versions of themselves. Everyone needs someone who will serve them selflessly.

For me, it was my coach. For you, it could be someone else. But whoever it is, create a relationship where your bond is built on service, trustworthiness, and support. This type of relationship is remarkable. This type of relationship will help you grow, will nurture and motivate you to do what you are destined to do in this world.

If you are in the field of serving others, then I can confidently say that having someone who serves as a coach, or a mentor, is of utmost importance, so that they may help you achieve your goals and also create a space where you can unravel about all the things that are affecting you in your work.

There are many relationships in the world, but the ones that leave you with a special value are the ones to keep close.

May Allah bless our relationships, strengthen our bonds, and use us to help each other.

Ameen.

MARRIAGE

Marriage is beautiful...If you are married to the right person, for the right reasons, and with the right understanding.

I shared my story of divorce with you, and I praise Allah for that experience. It is how I learned to find 'Mr. Right', so I wouldn't have to experience the same pain again. It is what I learned about marriage that taught me how to live and love in my marriage.

Marriage is another relationship in which many are blinded into. It is a choice one must make cautiously. The first thing to understand about marriage is 'why' someone gets married. It is essential to know that marriage is a sacred and divine bond which serves as an act of worship. It pleases Allah and by committing to this relationship we have the opportunity of a lifetime to please Allah (*Subhanahu-Wa-Ta'ala*).

Thus, like any other act that we commit to, we will be tested, and it is in these tests where we have the opportunity to practice patience and resilience.

Alhamdulillah, being ready for marriage requires a commitment to yourself and to Allah.

If you learn to put Allah first, and ask of Him, you will relieve yourself from setting false expectations from others. This is one way to avoid the pain and heartbreak in your marriage. You will learn more about how to depend and rely on Allah's guidance. This can only be done when one makes a conscious effort to increase their faith in Allah by learning about His attributes and His nature. It comes from turning to Him for all our needs and wants because it is He who has control of our affairs and who accepts our prayers. Strengthening our relationship with Allah means we have to be diligent in following His commands and following the footsteps of the Prophet (peace and blessings be upon him). It means doing things that Allah is pleased with. It is in this strengthening that our bond with Allah grows deeper, and it becomes easier for us to depend and expect from Him rather than people. People may let you down but Allah never will.

Another thing to understand is that, it is not only false expectations that bring about pain. They can most definitely be avoided, which in turn will save you from the heartbreak. However, once those expectations are set, individuals are still able to work through them. This helps increase the quality of life and lessens the hurt. In truth, it is the inability to work through differences that result in damaged marriages. It is what stirs up those bitter feelings between spouses. Marriage is a sacred bond, one which both individuals must honor. This means, that when a problem arises, both have to be keen, willing, sober, and open-minded to communicate and share their feelings. Both sides have to be prepared to make compromises, with the sole intention of ever-lasting their marriage.

Such problems and issues arising are but tests and trials, thus being patient and resilient through them will bear strength to the bond. Understanding this can save many marriages from failing with the bitterness that they do. Grasping this idea and practicing these skills of communicating, compromising, patience will help you in your marriage.

I often find that individuals are looking for spouses with characteristics they themselves don't carry. People are getting married without understanding what the building blocks of marriage really are.

Marriage is about becoming the person you want to attract and marry. If you want certain attributes in your spouse, you must first work to inhibit them in yourself. If there are certain things that are crucial to what you think will strengthen your marriage, then first ensure that you are practicing them yourself. Marriage is about understanding that everything you do is, in fact, an act of worship. Communication, compromise, and patience are just a handful of the many attributes which individuals ought to inhibit before they get married.

Marriage is about dialogue and conversation, about discussing what is acceptable and what is not. Marriage is about expressing love, affection, and gratitude to each other. It is about coming together in joy and trial, through good times and bad, and working through all the tribulations that arise. It is about accepting each other, sharing a vision, and growing together. Weak marriages are a result of not understanding these principles and foundations of marriage.

The above can only happen when one understands where they need to grow and what aspects of themselves they need to work on and improve. It can only happen when one understands marriage and begins to implement the characteristics that are necessary to make a marriage work. The few years after my first marriage and before my current one, I spent a lot of time preparing myself. I spent long nights in prayer to Allah, expressing my hearts desires. I spent time in natural environments, dwelling on what I really want. I understood my red-flags and what I sought in a spouse. I understood what I wanted in life and what I learned from my past. I upped my *Dua* and asked Allah for what I specifically want in my marriage and the qualities I want in my spouse, and by extension, my marriage. It is because of this process that I was able to settle down with the person I wanted. I realized that if I wanted a husband who feared Allah, I would constantly have to be cautious of not displeasing Allah. For example, if I wanted someone to give importance to his health then I would have to do so as well. Whatever attributes and things I wanted in him, I would have to ensure I have them in me as well.

Fast forward to today, I fall in love with my husband every day. He is my *Dua* fulfilled by Allah. He is the one relationship I can confidently say was an effort done right.

I am only happy because I understood Allah comes first and this gave me the knowledge and insight on how to attract 'Mr. Right'.

I have a course through which two sisters have successfully been able to find healthy marriages. It is a course based on the steps I took in my own life to prepare myself and settle down. You can find more information about it at the end of the book

Your future marriage starts today. If you are already married, then now is the time to focus on Allah and work on 'YOU' to attain a happy, joyful, *Barakah*-filled marriage.

This is the one relationship that Allah has blessed, so I pray Allah grants everyone a beautiful spouse, inside and out, and a happy marriage filled with His blessings.

ON THE JOURNEY OF BEING YOU

On the journey of being you, you must seek to fix the relationships around you. As Allah's creation, we are social creatures and surely, we cannot blossom without support from one another. So support each other. Maintain your ties. Beautify your bonds. This will help you learn from each other and start inhibiting characteristics so that you may become the best 'you' there will ever be.

REFLECTION QUESTIONS

1. What is the importance of the relationships around me and am I giving people their due right?

2. What is one action I can take today to improve my relationships?

3. What qualities can I change about me based on how others interact with me?

4. What are some steps I can take and encourage those around me (spouse, children, etc.), to take to strengthen ties with neighbors?

EXERCISE

I personally did this exercise before I got married and, *Alhamdulillah*, it really helped my spouse and I get to know each other better. Allah has blessed us with such unique traits and wants. In order to love someone, anyone, you have to understand HOW they want to be loved.

I would like to draw your attention to a wonderful tool I have personally used, and recommend everyone to use. It is a simple quiz, nothing fancy, but a powerful one, developed by a known personality, Dr. Gary Chapman, an author, a pastor, and a TV host. The quiz can be found on his website, www.5lovelanguages.com, and I also recommend reading his book, The 5 Love Languages.

This will help you learn and determine how you, truly and deeply, want to be loved. Then, you can start sharing this with others so they understand you.

Encourage others around you to complete this as well so you can strengthen your relationships. My love language is receiving gifts and physical affection.

What is yours?

My journey with Kulsoom really taught me about the importance of relationships. Knowing that having emotion is normal, I was able to translate my feelings into actions, rather than keep them contained. The overall improvement of my relationships reflected in my daily life. I am now able to better interact with others. It has helped me build myself, increase in my wisdom and widen my perspective.

— Duaa Saber, Canada

There was a time in my life when my relationships were causing me a lot of distress. Constant arguments with my husband and a little-to-zero relationship with Allah were manifesting horribly within me. After several sessions with Kulsoom, I slowly began to understand that when our relationship with Allah is on weak foundation, everything else crumbles, and this is exactly what was happening in my life. I understood how crucial it is to communicate feelings and expectations. Thank you Kulsoom for being that guiding light.

— Aisha, United States of America

Be a 'feeler' so you can understand your feelings and of those around you

SELF CARE

If you don't take control of your life,
someone else will

WHEN WOMEN PUT THEMSELVES LAST

I have learned that women all around the world have one thing in common. It doesn't matter what age they are or what culture they belong to, the struggle is often the same. I find women to be so powerful and resilient. So beautiful by Allah's incomparable design. They are also warriors in life, facing their own battles and I have come across many strong women throughout my life, my mother being one of them. However, in this love for others, I find that women forget themselves.

We forget that we are delicate flowers that need to be nurtured. We forget that we need love and affection to bloom. We forget the passions we once wanted to pursue. My mother fits into these words like a key to a lock. I have seen her bloom throughout the years. She has worked hard to raise us and nurture us. She has grown in her capacity to absorb trials and learn from them. However, despite this blooming, I have also seen her wither away.

She loved us. She adored us. Her desire to hold us close and protect us became the purpose of all that she wanted to do in her life. She drenched in this purpose so much that she had almost forgotten about her own well-being. She had almost forgotten that the beautifully defined lines that come with age also need to be taken care of. She forgets that her health has frivoled and that it demands her attention. She put herself ultimately last so that we could smile and enjoy the luxuries of this world. She continues to this day, to give everyone around her importance, thinking that this would fulfill her, and that it was her duty and obligation to the world.

She too, like a little girl, once had big dreams. She has many fine skills and talents. She had goals and aspirations, all to be lost to what we call life. She's proud of the children she has raised and the life she has created. Her life has become wonderful based on the sacrifices she made, but somewhere deep down, she knows she could've achieved more had she taken care of herself. Had she worked on herself the way you and I ought to.

It saddens me when I think about so many women who have lost out on achieving their dreams in a similar manner. My heart aches because I know they are capable of so much more. I can feel the pain that many carry and are unable to express because they assume they are being selfish. Let me remind you, it is not selfish. It is not selfish to take care of yourself, nurture yourself, and look after your mind, body, and soul. Yes, many commit to what they do, happily and consciously, but what about those who are smiling out of a compromise that life pushed on them. And they have gone too far, unable to come back. It makes me sad because this is the reality of many women, many mothers. Putting themselves last.

I once conducted a workshop packed with beautiful mothers. As I waited to begin my talk, I took a moment to study all the faces in the room. They all displayed anxious expressions for what I was about to unfold. Some were nervously glancing about. Others were smiling and talking amongst themselves, but behind those smiles, I could see hardened years of struggles. Behind those eyes, I could see many tears, shed over what they wished their life could be. As strange as it may sound, I was inspired. It was a challenge for me, but a bigger challenge on them, and I knew, if they found success, no one in that room would be happier than I.

As I walked up to the podium I sensed their

eagerness, on edge, awaiting some words of wisdom, anticipating something extraordinary from me. Something that would ease their path. A solution, perhaps a quick-fix to all their problems.

When I spoke, I felt the atmosphere in the room change. There was no concealing their befuddled expressions when I told them that the solution to their problems was to put themselves first.

Eyes widened, shoulders tensed, and they shifted in their seats with discomfort. It was a foreign concept; one which they thought may never be cultivated. I assured them, with all the energy I could muster, that it could.

It is difficult. It is challenging. It is tedious. It takes determination to achieve, but it can be achieved. Once you realize that there is a world out there beyond the one you are living, it can be achieved. Your goals and ambitions matter. You matter. Amongst the crowd and the people you are taking care of, YOU MATTER.

It is a process, and you have to start somewhere, and that somewhere is here. Start with some important realizations and actions, and watch how you blossom into who you are meant to be.

I left that room with that simple thought, reminding myself of my purpose in this world. I want to make a difference in the lives of everyone I meet, in one way or another. I want to empower the women of our *Ummah* to become the extraordinary women they already are. Really help them bring the best versions of themselves out. But first, I have to create a dialogue about self-care. This is where we are lacking.

This isn't just for mothers. It's for everyone. I have seen my own clients go through it, my own family and friends. I experienced falling into it when I touched the brinks of motherhood – I had put myself last without a second thought. But I caught myself. I caught myself because I realized, that if I were to lose myself, then I won't be able to serve Allah to the best of my ability. I won't be able to meet my full potential. I won't be able to accomplish all that my heart desires. I will be in this endless race where I will always lose, and I want to win. This is why I realized I must focus on myself. My mind, body, and soul. Self-care doesn't have come at the expense of your family or the *Ummah*, rather self-care relates to considering all these aspects, understanding and carrying out our responsibilities and obligations, but also maintaining a balance between them and ourselves.

How many people do you know are battling with self-care? Are YOU one of them?

CULTIVATING SELF-CARE

We hear about self-care, but do we cultivate it? Do we really know what it means to care for our mind, body, and soul? I believe we know. We have the answers. They're with us, around us. They lie at the deepest core of our hearts because we know what it is that we need to prosper. It just takes some reflection and deep-digging to bring them to the surface. Our religion teaches us. We just don't practice it. We don't reason with it and as a result, we steer further away from who we are meant to be and do. We love so deeply and passionately, but we forget that we deserve love too, not just from others but from ourselves as well. Yes, we deserve love. Allah created us this way and so in order to flourish, we have to nurture ourselves. We have to free ourselves from the shackles of this world and free ourselves from attaching our self-worth to others.

Not to mistake self-care for embarking on an endless race of individualistic desires, but to focus on yourself so that you can be in a better place to serve Allah, and to serve others.

When a woman is younger, she wants to

please her parents and elders around her so she works day and night in desperate search of their approval.

Why?

So society will be pleased with her, and her parents will be proud, and that will see her married to a 'respectable' family or build her career to 'greatness' and highest 'success'.

When she is younger, society pressures her to look and act in a manner that would make her look 'attractive' and gain her 'popularity' within said society.

When she is a young adult, she cares for her friends and colleagues because that will deem her 'popular' so she goes out of her way to please them instead of using this ripe time to nurture her soul.

When she becomes a wife, the cycle is the same. She does everything to keep her husband happy not uttering a word about her wants, needs, and desires.

The cycle continues endlessly. Every young girl enters this world in the same manner. Day in and day out, she puts others first. She forgets that Allah has to come first for her to attain success in anything. She forgets that her body has rights over her. She forgets that if she doesn't nurture her mind and heart, she will have nothing to fall back on. Others will progress, and she will stay in the same place, unhappy.

It's okay to love. It's okay to put others first at times. It's okay to care and serve. To give and compromise. It's all okay. What's not okay is forgetting where you fit into this puzzle. That balance is what we must seek to bring back in our lives, so we can avoid the unhappiness we may face without it.

On the journey of being you, you must focus on your heart and soul. You have to fill it with the remembrance of Allah.

Allah says in the Qur'an, *Soorah Al-Baqarah Ayah 152: "Therefore remember Me, I will remember you and be grateful to Me and never be ungrateful to Me".*

You have to fix your prayers and your relationship with the Qur'an. You must seek knowledge of this religion. This is the only way you will be able to stand up for what is right, and attain that special place in *Jannah* (paradise). If you prioritize this, all your other relationships will prosper. This is self-care.

On the journey of being you, you have to find time for your body. You must strengthen it with the right food and exercise. This is how you will live the rest of your life happily and, *In'sha'Allah*, pain-free. This is self-care.

On the journey of being you, you must exercise your intellect. Seek knowledge about this religion and other aspects of life. Do something to give back to the *Ummah*. Do something you love, so you can maintain your individuality. Spend time with yourself, so can you learn about yourself, what you want and need. This is self-care.

See, we think that by putting others first, we will be happy and Allah will be pleased. Allah will always be pleased with every sacrifice you make. However, often when you put others first you forget to worship Allah. You forget to cleanse your heart. You forget about your talents and how to contribute to the *Ummah*. In the end, neither you, nor Allah, is particularly happy. Is this the life you want?

This is what taking care of your mind, body and soul really means. Catering to each of them in a unique way.

Now don't get me wrong. We should always be at the service of others, right at the forefront.

We should run to help those in need. We should think about what people around us want. The Prophet (peace and blessings be upon him) was the best of mankind, and he was always at the service of others. But not at the expense of your mind, body, and soul. When you do this, you're doing a disservice to others. You'll fall short of taking care of others when you haven't taken care of yourself.

Therefore, like the women I have met, you will be exhausted, bitter, and unhappy.

The journey of being you, starts now. It starts with the realization that you are important. You deserve greatness. You deserve the best. So take the steps necessary and cultivate self-care for your mind, body, and soul, and watch how you bloom into a beautiful, breathtaking rose. You are so kind to others. It's time to be kind to yourself.

ON THE JOURNEY OF BEING YOU

On the journey of being you, realize that you matter. When you cater to yourself you are automatically catering to Allah, your mind and your body. When you connect with these aspects you will be whole. You will become the best version of you that will ever live.

REFLECTION QUESTIONS

1. What are some of my passions in life? Things that I love to do?

2. How can I achieve them?

3. How can I communicate my feelings to the people around me so they can support me towards achieving my goals?

4. What do I need to cultivate to be my best self?

EXERCISE

CONTEMPLATE IN SILENCE

I have always been someone in tune with my emotions. I lost this along the way but regained it simply by sitting with myself. Focusing on my heart, in silence.

This is how I am able to see my flaws and work on them. This is how I can reflect on the beautiful world that Allah has created and ponder upon my existence.

There is something magnificent about silence. It surfaces the words that you wouldn't otherwise be able to hear in all the noise. Prophet Muhammad (peace be upon him) was also found, many times, meditating and contemplating in silence. He spent countless hours in the solitude of cave of Hira.

We live in a busy world, and so this exercise is all about timing out. Sitting in silence. Focusing on your thoughts. This will help you come to realize all that you are confused about in this life. It will help you realize which areas of your life you need to work on. It will help you get in tune with yourself, your emotions, and Allah. For me, this is the ultimate form of self-care.

Put this book down and find somewhere in your home, or outside, and practice silence. Sit there and watch the trees. Reflect on nature and let the silence do the talking.

I have practiced self-care with Kulsoom's help by first changing my mindset about what self-care means to me. For me, I always associated self-care with being selfish, but I had to understand that if my glass is empty then I cannot be of use to other people, my family and friends. So changing my mindset and taking an active approach to self-healing and self-love has allowed me to put myself first. I have learned that I am actually being of service to other people by being of service to myself.

Self-care has changed my life by making me more patient and practice kindness to myself. I have learned to slow down and set time out for myself. I have learned that healing takes time and also to set boundaries, and that the word NO is not a bad thing but actually a part of the journey of self-care. – Hibaq Adam, Canada

I had been hearing about self-care for some time but I didn't really know what it meant until I started my coaching sessions with Kulsoom. When I started to practice self-care I didn't know what to do at all. With help, I was able to figure some of it out and I continue to learn more as time goes on. I am no master at it yet, but I understand the value of self-care and I am trying to make it a daily habit.

I realized that setting aside time for myself had a good impact on my mood and daily interactions and if I wasn't able to set time aside then I'd feel agitated, moody and avoid everyone. I still go through days when I am not practicing self-care and I immediately know that I need to do something that makes me feel good or at peace. – Anika Ahmed, Canada

Growth requires nurturing thyself

CONFIDENCE

You will become what you believe about
yourself

MY CONFIDENCE LACKED

I have been told many times that I am confident. I have made my attempts at embodying confidence. I walk with my head held high, not out of pride, but because I accept who I am in my attempts to become who I am meant to be. How can I have pride when I am merely a servant of Allah? I bow to my Lord in submission, and while that may seem like I lack self-esteem, it is my belief that this is a form of modesty and humility. It shows that there is someone who is greater than us all. He deserves our respect, love, and humility. I cannot be unhappy about what Allah made me and chose for me. My confidence stems from His love for me and everything he has created in this world.

So, yes, if this is confidence, then I am confident. However, let me assure you, that there are times when my confidence has sunk to depths which I could not fathom. There are times when I have doubted everything about myself.

I had someone significant in my life (who is no longer there) tell me, since I was a little girl, that I am not good enough. Therefore, I believed, with my fragile heart, that I wasn't. I developed a sense of hatred for myself. I grew up always feeling misplaced, as if I didn't belong to this world of beauty and perfection. I felt I needed the approval of others, to be pretty.

'You're beautiful.'

'You're cute.'

These are the words I wanted to hear... This is how I spent those years of my life, when I should have been enjoying every moment of joy as a youth. I remember some days when all my young heart wanted was to feel...to be wanted, to be loved. I wanted someone to recognize my existence and appreciate me. I wanted to feel special so I could believe that I am. I didn't think I would ever last in a relationship because again, I didn't think I had what it took to make it work. I was scared of entering any relationship out of the fear of being rejected. I even thought about hurting myself because the pressure society put on me was too much to bear sometimes.

The illusion created, that if you're not a certain weight, certain skin color, certain height or anything according to society's standards, you will never feel good enough. They won't let you. But the thing is, you have to push society back. You will never be able to please them because the same society that tells you, for example, you're too fat, will also tell someone else they're too thin. There's no end to it. You can scream. You can cry. You can even die for it, but it makes no impact on them.

The change has to come from you. You have to take a stand and protect your heart. Protect yourself. I was a victim of this. I was taller than my age at fourteen. Darker than what an average Pakistani apparently should be. As I grew up I realized that fourteen-year-olds are beautiful in all shapes and sizes. They shouldn't be defined by what they should be, but rather for who they are. There is no one number that fits all. I realized that the world comes in all different colors. Women are of many types. All beautiful. It's Allah's creation. They can't be anything less than majestic. As I looked around, I realized Allah made us beautiful in different ways and it is this beauty that we have to embody, understand, and give out to the world.

Therefore, I made a decision. I put my hands up and asked Allah for assistance, and thus empowered myself against society. I cleansed my mind and heart of the dirt that it was riddled with, molding me into who I am not. I started seeking approval from myself and accepting the way Allah made me. I realized that because I will never be able to please others, the only one I have to please is Allah. I may never fit the standards set by others, so I started imitating the pious people of the past and emulating our beloved Prophet (peace be upon him). This is how I obtained my confidence. Being content with how Allah made me. So yes, if you look at me now, I seem confident, but the battle within myself continues. Every. Single. Day.

You know why? Because society still exists. The voices are still there. So, I, like others, fight every single day to not let society define us. We struggle to be our unique individual selves. We work from the inside out. We cleanse our minds and our hearts. Because this is what matters. Truly, this is how we will become the best versions of ourselves. When we accept who we are and own it. This is confidence.

BEING YOU

I wrote this book with a clear purpose. I want to help YOU become the best version of yourself. Work towards the best you there can be. We have it. We have it in us to be the best slaves of Allah. We have it in us to empower ourselves and those around us. We have it in us to make a difference in this world. I believe you have it. So believe in yourself. That's when you will conquer all.

How many times do we feel unhappy with ourselves when we look at someone on TV? We envy them and yearn to be like them. How many times does ungratefulness stir up, after seeing someone on social media living their 'best life'? We want what they have, not realizing that they too carry pain behind their smiles. Media will be the destruction of us. It will destroy us if we continue to compare ourselves to others. It will destroy us if we become dumbfounded into believing that people are perfect. We may believe that their lives are perfect. I can assure you, that is not the case.

It may sound simple but you will only be great if you please Allah, connect with your core and bring your best self out.. That is what you are good at and what you are raw at.

Be comfortable with yourself. Whoever that is. It is only when you accept yourself that you can grow. It is only when you accept who you are that you can work on your flaws. If we live denying who we are and what's within our hearts, how will we ever learn who we are meant to be? Set standards for yourself and work on that. The key to attaining confidence is putting your trust in Allah after you have decided to do something. Be confident in His ability to help you with your plans, and help you achieve success. This is a type of confidence that will help you achieve things you only imagined.

"Then, when you have decided on a course of action, put your trust in Allah; Allah loves those who put their trust in Him. If Allah helps you (believers), no one can overcome you. If he forsakes you, who else can help you? Believers should put their trust in Allah"
[Soorah Aal-e-Imran, Ayah 159-160].

We are not meant to be perfect, so yearning

for that will leave you at loss. We are perfect in our imperfections.

See, what we fail to understand, is that we should have standards and there is nothing wrong in becoming a better version of yourself, but the definition of what is better has to come from you. It has to come from what Allah wants from you. It has to come from the deepest parts of your heart. The standards have to come from you. From within. Where your heart is connected to Allah. We can only become that better person when we accept who we are today. You don't have to like it, just accept it. Acceptance will help you take the necessary steps to change. It will push you to embark on a journey so profound, that by the end of it, you will be awed at the person you have become and continue to be every single day.

Whether you have anger, arrogance, hypocrisy, lack of courage, whatever it is. Accept it and move away from it. Move to the person YOU want to become, not who others want you to be.

This is the recipe for being authentic. Being raw. Being you.

THE DETRIMENTS OF SOCIAL MEDIA

Our lives have taken a complete turn since the introduction of Social Networking and Media, resulting in a dramatic decrease in actual human interaction and by extension, diminishing our abilities to interact and maintain relationships built on solid foundations.

How many times do we seek approval from what we put out to this digital world?

For that 'Like', that 'Reaction', or 'Comment' or 'Private message'.

It is an endless and repetitive cycle, a plague affecting so many, right from a young and tender age.

I will say that social media has its benefits if used for the right reasons, because social media, like anything else, is what you make of it. Anything consumed in excess can become poison, and Social Media is no different.

It is not meant to be a place where you allow 'likes' and 'comments' to define your self-worth. It is not a place where the number of followers should determine how great of an impact you have. While I may not be able to tell you that the way you are using it is wrong, you best know yourself, so ask yourself this: If social media didn't exist, would you still feel good about yourself and your life? If social media didn't exist, would you still make the efforts to have an impact on the world?

Ask yourself and be true to this reflection.

Don't allow social media to define you. Do not allow your life to be compared to those of others. Everyone is struggling in one way, shape, or form, and what is shown on social media isn't even half of it, it's a small glimpse, just the beautified parts.

Don't allow your confidence to tremble from it. Allow it to assist you as you change the world around you.

ON THE JOURNEY OF BEING YOU

On the journey of being you, you must strive to be your best-self by accepting who you are in this very moment and owning it. Own it in such a way, that it leaves you inspired to become the best version of yourself. Cultivate words that encourage you, not let you down.

REFLECTION QUESTIONS

1. Whom do I compare myself to, and is this healthy for me?

2. What hinders my confidence, and what are some of the things I can do to build it?

3. What does it mean to love myself? How do I continue to develop myself?

4. How will confidence help me achieve my overall vision in life?

EXERCISE

AFFIRMATIONS

Ever since I was a teenager, I was always keen on reading affirmations. They made me feel good. They gave me reassurance. I read them every day until I became them.

A lot of what we go through is because of how we speak to ourselves. We are so kind to others, and unknowingly unkind to ourselves. Confidence comes from within. Focus on your language towards yourself. Create your own affirmations.

For this exercise make a list of things you are insecure about. It could be your weight, your looks, your career, anything.

Take each thing you wrote above and write down the exact opposite. For example, if you wrote 'I am overweight', write down 'I am beautiful the way I am'. If you wrote 'I am unworthy', write down 'I am worthy of more than I can imagine'.

Take this list and read it every day. I promise you, this will make a difference.

Here are some affirmations to get you

started:

I am beautiful

I am worthy of all good

I am capable of more than I deem my self

I am where I am supposed to be in life

Allah loves me

I am destined for greatness

Nothing about what I say above is half-hearted. I genuinely believe each of you is worthy of so much greatness. It's just a matter of you believing it and cultivating it.

I grew up with Islamophobia and racism. In all these occurrences, people's perception of me influenced my actions. "Why do you think that is?" Kulsoom asked me during my life coaching sessions. "Your belief in yourself should be consistent, regardless of how anyone looks at you." Those words unlocked a new perspective, in which I realized that other's thoughts and behaviors were beyond my control. It begun a journey of creating affirmations and eventually

learning to believe myself. I used to live a life where confidence was dependent on external, temporary factors such as appearance or income status. Through Kulsoom, I learned that real confidence was so much more than that. It was a belief in God, an internal set of values and the knowledge that we are human and we are doing our best

— Saamiyah Ali, Canada

Firstly I would say that confidence is a journey and a process; just like many other aspects of life. It does not happen overnight, and it requires practice. I developed confidence (and honestly still developing it) because Allah gifted it to me when He answered my Dua. Some of the things I did in the process are:

1. I made Dua for it. Nothing in this world happens solely because of you and your actions alone. Action is necessary, but Dua is essential.

2. Mindset. Breaking the 'limitation belief' I had painted myself with since my childhood. Mainly, the 'what if', 'I cant' and 'I am not good enough'. One particular exercise I did with Kulsoom, that impacted my confidence the most, was setting my standard. When I began to establish what beauty, success or confidence means to me (and not society), I began to see the world and myself from my own lens, and not the lenses of others. How I saw myself mattered more than how others saw me.

3. Action – Alhamdulillah, my divorce was one of the ways Allah pushed me in the direction of taking ownership of my life, and my confidence began building from thereon. Some of the actions I took earlier on were: I traveled with total strangers (Alhamdulillah, in Malaysia we have many 'sisters solo travel' groups). I began dating myself, connecting with myself, and I spoke up about my ideas and thoughts more in classes and conferences that I attended by myself (without friends- I started making new friends from the events I would attend). 'I have no friends and no one to go with' had been my excuse for a long time. What these solo actions did - They challenged and pushed me out of my comfort zone. And now the boundary of what is comfortable (and less scary) has grown. We are more confident with what we are comfortable. How overall confidence makes a difference in my life? I speak up more - my ideas, my emotions, and boundaries helped me to grow my personal strength. My relationships with others and my career as well. I no longer look down on myself. I started doing things I never thought I could do.

Life became more colorful for me.

— Jahn Mokhtar, Malaysia

Be cautious of the words you are using to describe yourself

May Allah bless you for reading this book, and bless you in your efforts to work on yourself and become the best 'you' this world will ever see.

May Allah shower his mercy upon us, make us amongst those with whom He is pleased, and allow us to follow in the footsteps of our beloved Prophet (peace and blessings be upon him).

If you have benefited from this book, reach out to me.

I would love to hear from you.

Thank you for listening...

GLOSSARY

Abaya – a full length and loose outer garment worn by Muslim women

Alhamdulillah – All praise is to Allah

Allah – God. Creator of the universe.

Ayah – Verse

Barakah – Blessing

Dua – invocation; supplication; to ask of Allah

Dunya – The World

Eid – Muslim day of celebration, twice every Lunar year, at the end of Ramadhan and on the Tenth day of Pilgrimage

Fajr – The dawn prayer

Hijab – A headscarf or Head-covering. Also referred to the concept of covering oneself from the world outside and temptation inside.

In'sha'Allah – If Allah wills

Jannah - Paradise

Khul'ua – Islamic legal divorce stipulated by the female

Muslimah – A Muslim woman

Nikah – marriage under Islamic law

Quran – The Islamic Holy Book; The word of Allah

Shaykh – a learned leader in a Muslim community or organization

Soorah - Chapter

Subhanahu-Wa-Ta'ala – The most Glorified, the most High

Ummah – The Islamic community as a whole

ABOUT THE AUTHOR

Kulsoom Kazim is a high-performance coach and a gifted motivational speaker. She graduated from York University, Ontario, with an Honors Degree in Psychology and a heart full of passion to change the world.

As of publishing her debut, Be You, is in the midst of completing her Islamic degree at Mishkah University and currently working towards her *Ijazah* in *Quran* and *Tajweed*.

She hosts and also participates in various motivational and self-help workshops, and conducts lectures to inspire woman around the globe.

Her main goal is to impact the hearts of women and help them become their best-self, so we can make the *Ummah* a better place.

She lives in Ontario, Canada with her husband and cat, and is often found enjoying nature and supporting local Muslim organizations.

Her doors are always open and welcome to anyone who calls on her. The best way to reach out to her is through:

 www.kulsoomkazim.com

 kulsoomlifecoach@gmail.com

 @kulsoomlifecoach

 @kulsoomlifecoach

Printed in Great Britain
by Amazon